LOS ANGELES & SOUTHERN CALIFORNIA

GALLERY BOOKS
An Imprint of W. H. Smith Publishers Inc.
112 Madison Avenue
New York City 10016

Southern California's main geological features, aside from its coastline, are two mountain ranges and the great Central Valley that lies between them. The mountains of the Coastal Range are generally below 4,000 feet, while the inland peaks of the Sierra Nevada rise to 14,000 feet.

Most of Southern California has an arid, almost subtropical climate. The heat of the day is fanned by prevailing westerly winds and the change in seasons often goes unnoticed. There is no doubt that the year-round sun and cooling breezes have drawn many to Southern California. Few places outside of this region share such good fortune when it comes to blue skies and dry, warm weather. In fact, less than one percent of the earth's surface enjoys such an ideal climate, making Southern California a very special place.

Other attractions also bring people here. The coastal highway outside of Monterey provides a scenic and peaceful tour of Southern California. Small communities, wind-swept hills, and the Pacific Ocean can all be found on this road in a harmonious, balanced setting.

South on this route stands a "castle" on a hill. With zebras surrounding it, what first appears to be an optical illusion turns out to be real: the San Simeon estate of William Randolph Hearst, the infamous newspaper publisher.

Preceding page: *The Santa Barbara Mission sits on a hilltop overlooking the town. Surrounded by pepper trees and shrubs, its chapel is still used by the parish of Santa Barbara.* This page: *The terrace surrounding the Griffith Observatory is a good place to view Los Angeles. From a distance, the lights of the city look like sparkling jewels on a black background.*

Above, left to right: *Westwood Village is the shopping, cinema, and restaurant center of the University of California in Los Angeles. The Farmer's Market in West Hollywood is considered the world's largest cafeteria and indoor/outdoor grocery. Below: One of Los Angeles' most notable buildings is the Pan-Pacific Auditorium, which bears an art deco façade.*

The Los Angeles Memorial Coliseum, sporting the five linked Olympic rings over its entrance, was the site of the 1984 summer games.
Below: *An Olympic mural on the side of an overpass has a three-dimensional look to it.*

Preceding page: *Dodger Stadium.* This page, above: *The Rose Bowl in Pasadena is known as a football venue, although it served as the Olympic soccer site in 1984.* Below: *The Forum is Los Angeles' premier showplace for sports and entertainment.*

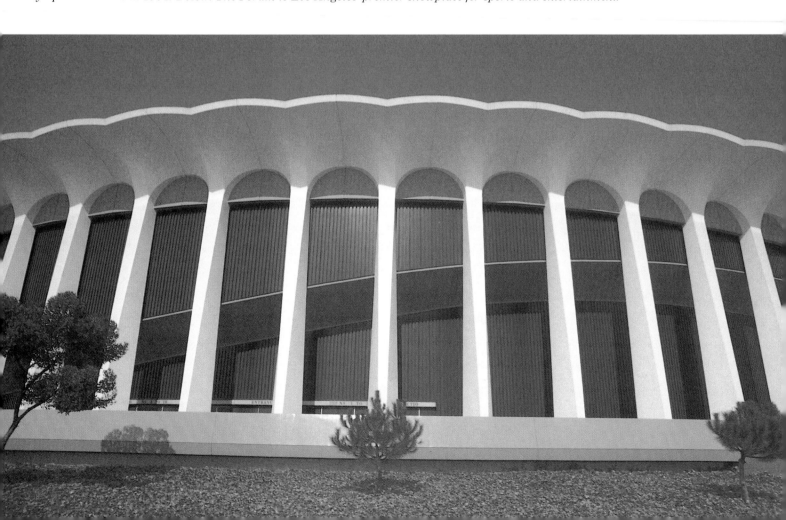

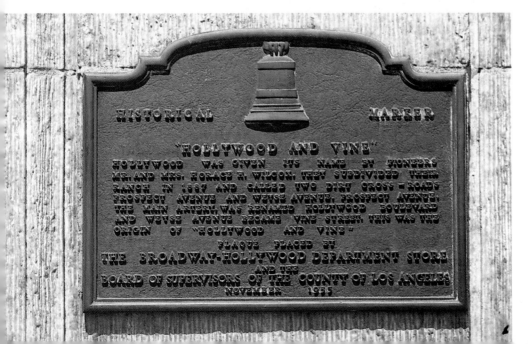

South of Venice, in the greater Los Angeles area, is Marina del Rey. It has the largest man-made pleasure boat harbor on the Pacific coast—more than ten thousand boats of all shapes and sizes are moored here.

Coming into Los Angeles can be a confusing experience. It's hard to tell where it begins and ends due to the urban sprawl along the coast and throughout the valley. Numerous communities have been tacked onto the city proper and have become integral parts of Los Angeles, including Beverly Hills and Burbank, which are independently incorporated.

Stretching inland from the Pacific—over four hundred square miles—Los Angeles was the first major city to build outwards instead of up. With the city's history of earthquakes, it is only recently that carefully designed skyscrapers have been built.

In keeping pace with the rest of the world, Los Angeles' architecture is a combination of the modern, material, and artistic. Fast freeways, glass and chrome buildings, and contemporary artwork cover the city. Some old sections of town remain intact, but most have given way to modern structures.

This page, top to bottom: *The famous Hollywood sign originally read "Hollywoodland," after the residential area to the north of Hollywood where it sits. The corner of Hollywood and Vine is ordinary in looks but rich in history, thanks to the many stars who've crossed the intersection. A plaque at the site tells of its origin.*

Above, left to right: *The Hollywood Bowl is a popular place for pop concerts and operas. Mann's Chinese Theater is a combination of authentic and reproduced Chinese decor. Two of its columns supposedly came from a Ming Dynasty temple.* Below: *Mann's Chinese Theater is famous for its forecourt, which contains the handprints and footprints of Hollywood's greatest stars.*

Los Angeles' humble beginnings, however, can still be seen in historic Pueblo de Los Angeles at the edge of downtown. Here, cobblestoned streets and adobes mark the city's Spanish and Mexican roots. Olvera Street is the main pedestrian lane in the Pueblo, with artisans, shops, and restaurants, both Mexican and Californian.

In the north end of town is another historical district—one that lives on in the mind rather than in the streets. At one time, Hollywood was considered to be the movie capital of the world. Over the years, many of the studios moved to the nearby San Fernando Valley. The area is now a sort of Times Square of the West, its days of glamorous movie stars long since gone.

Not far from Hollywood, straddling the eastern end of the Santa Monica Mountains, is Griffith Park. This is one of the largest municipal parks in the country, stretching over four thousand acres of flat and mountainous land.

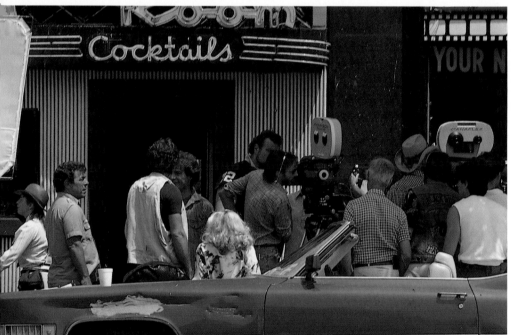

This page, top to bottom: *Universal Studios is the largest studio in the world, with over five hundred buildings spread across 420 acres of land. A common sight on the studio lot and on the street is moviemaking in action. Observers can often watch a film in the making.* Opposite: *Beverly Hills is its own municipality, even though it is surrounded by Los Angeles. For a small town, its city hall is quite grand, but so are many of the buildings in this wealthy community.*

Griffith Park is home to the Los Angeles Zoo, the Griffith Observatory and Planetarium, and Ferndell, where New Zealand horticulturalists have planted ferns from around the world. There is also a natural canyon amphitheater, known as the Greek Theater, which is a popular place for drama, music, and dance performances.

For those who are interested in star gazing and window shopping, Beverly Hills is the place to go. Surrounded by Los Angeles, Beverly Hills has fought to remain a separate municipality and has its own courthouse, police force, and mayor.

The shops on Rodeo Drive make up one of the most exclusive retail areas in the world and are frequented by the rich and famous of Beverly Hills. Window shoppers and tourists are not an uncommon sight.

Many of the houses in Beverly Hills could easily be called mansions. They vary in style and are the homes of many television and movie stars. The grounds of these homes are well worth seeing, since many of them are carefully tended by full-time gardeners.

In addition to being a bustling business center, Los Angeles is a center for the arts.

This page, top to bottom: *This Spanish-style house is just one of many beautiful homes in the glens, canyons, and hillsides of Beverly Hills. Many stars call Beverly Hills home, as do Southern California's most prestigious hotels, restaurants, and stores. Among the palatial homes of Beverly Hills are a few that don't quite fit the mold, like the Willat House, better known as the "witch house," for its scary looks.*

Dance, drama, and musical performances have a variety of venues to choose from, including indoor and outdoor stages. Fine art is also well represented, with a number of museums, galleries, and exhibition halls that offer permanent and traveling shows.

South of downtown, on the water, is Long Beach, a pedestrian-friendly community with a mall and boardwalk running from downtown to the shoreline. A number of industries drive this community: shipping, naval operations, oil, conventions, and tourism. In addition to having the busiest port on the West Coast, Long Beach has one of the largest and most attractive convention centers in the country. Two unusual tourist attractions line Long Beach's piers: the Queen Mary oceanliner and the Spruce Goose, Howard Hughes' massive wooden plane. Thanks to careful city planning, Long Beach successfully hosts all of these activities.

This page, top to bottom: *Beverly Hills' Rodeo Drive is one of the country's most exclusive and pricey shopping areas. The Beverly Center is a covered shopping complex on Rodeo Drive that houses a number of stores and restaurants, including the Hard Rock Cafe, a popular spot for celebrity events. Cafes, trend-setting boutiques, and expensive cars line Rodeo Drive.*

Forest Lawn Cemetery is known for being the liveliest cemetery in the world. Its "sacred gardens" offer many attractions, including the Great Mausoleum, where Clark Gable and Jean Harlow are buried. Left: Forest Lawn is also a place for the living; people often come here to get married or to christen their children.

Known by many as an "American Riviera," Malibu attracts thousands of yearly visitors, as well as a number of television and movie stars who make this Pacific strip their home. Right: Surfers catch a wave off the shores of Malibu.

Santa Monica, popular for sportfishing, has been a resort town since the late 1800's. Below: Santa Monica has a colorful municipal pier surrounded by well-groomed beaches. People of all ages gather here to swim, sunbathe, and walk the pier. Opposite: One of Santa Monica's landmarks is the Singing Beach Chair, a whimsical structure with organ pipes built into its back.

The oceanside community of Venice was originally built to resemble its Italian namesake. The discovery of oil off its shores changed its appearance, although it still retains some of its canals and one-lane bridges. *Left:* Today, Venice is famous for its boardwalk, with colorful music and colorful people walking and roller-skating along its promenade.

This page, clockwise: *The Arco Center exemplifies Long Beach's prosperous economy. Marina Del Rey is the largest small-craft harbor in the world. Sailboats slice the water as the wind kicks up during Long Beach Race Week.*

South of Long Beach is Orange County, home of the first large-scale fantasy theme park, Disneyland. Built in the 1950's, it is one of the biggest tourist attractions in Southern California. More recently, other specialty parks and special-interest museums have opened up, making much of this county a big entertainment center.

Disneyland is a special treat for young and old alike. Everyone has a favorite attraction and many prefer the park at night, with its glittering lights and fireworks.

Orange County also has a number of beaches that are meccas for sun worshippers and surfers. Huntington Beach is considered by many surfers to be "the capital," since it is the home of the summer international surfing competition. Most of these intrepid wave riders show up in the early morning or evening to avoid swimmers and sunbathers.

Newport Beach boasts opulent homes and handsome yachts. Thousands of pleasure boats use the harbor at Balboa Peninsula, a narrow strip of sand stretching out to sea. Across the bridge is Lido Island, a fashionable residential area where every waterfront home has a boat.

Down the coast from Newport Beach, on Pacific Highway South, is Laguna Beach, Southern California's prominent art colony where ceramic art was pioneered. Many artisans and artists were flourishing here well before they began flocking to New York City's Greenwich Village.

Next to the Queen Mary, under an aluminum dome, is Howard Hughes' 200-ton Spruce Goose, which still holds the record for being the largest plane ever built.

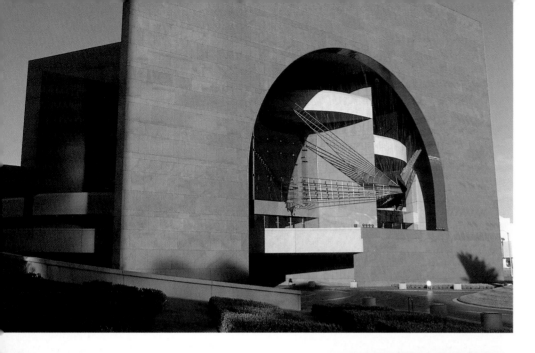

Southern California's last big city before the Mexican border is San Diego. The Spanish influence returns here with a lovely "Old Town" that has many white, stucco structures with red-tiled roofs. The "Mother of Missions" is also here, Mission San Diego de Alcala. This was the first of 21 missions to be built throughout the state.

San Diego is famous for its zoo and its beautiful harbor. Vast, natural, and nearly landlocked, the San Diego Harbor is one of the world's best deepwater anchorages. Vessels of all sizes are moored here, including the Navy's largest fleet of ships.

San Diego is California's third largest city, but its relaxed pace belies its size. Everything seems slower here, which makes it a particularly appealing city for young families and retired people. Expansive parks and university campuses offer space where people can enjoy themselves. Nearby La Jolla has broad beaches for sunning and swimming.

The Southern California desert is also a land of variety. Palm Springs lies about a hundred miles east of Los Angeles where the San Jacinto Mountains meet the desert floor. Known as the golf capital of the world, Palm Springs is covered with golf courses.

This page, top to bottom: *The Orange County Performing Arts Center, situated on five acres, is the area's first major theater complex. The Santa Anita Park racetrack in Arcadia is known for its elaborate infields, complete with ponds and decorative shrubbery. The glass-paneled Crystal Cathedral in Garden Grove evokes a light, airy feeling.*

When the sun goes down, Anaheim's Disneyland lights up with fireworks at its castle entrance. Inside, neon lights and old-fashioned streetlamps warm the scene. Below: The Mark Twain Steamboat ride in Frontierland.

Balboa Pavilion on Catalina Island is a restored Victorian landmark and serves as a terminal for harbor boats. Below: Mission San Miguel is one of 21 missions established by the Franciscan order of Catholic priests. Opposite, clockwise: The remains of some of the oldest buildings in California are on the grounds of the Mission San Juan Capistrano. Destroyed by an earthquake, the ruins provide a nesting place for swallows and other birds. Birds are treated with respect at the Mission San Juan Capistrano; a fountain on the grounds has even been dedicated to pigeons.

Laguna Beach is best known as an artist's colony—the Greenwich Village of the West. Its sandy beaches and rolling waves also draw surfers. Below: Newport Beach is a relaxed resort town with a yacht harbor.

Mission San Luis Rey is one of the best restored missions in the 21 mission chain. Known for its artistic façade, it sits on a hill overlooking a valley. Below: Mission San Luis Rey was the largest and most populous Indian mission in America. Now a seminary, it is open to the public.

A wooden fish shanty sits on a pier at Seaport Village on the San Diego Bay.
Opposite: San Diego has one of the most famous harbors in the world. About
six thousand pleasure boats are moored here, along with the United States Navy
Pacific submarine fleet and an array of warships.

To the north of Palm Springs is Death Valley. Situated along the California/Nevada border, it covers two million acres of the Mojave desert. At 262 feet below sea level, the town of Bad Water is the lowest point in the country. Death Valley acquired its unfriendly name from parties of travelers whose horses and cattle perished in its arid environment. During the Gold Rush, some prospectors took this route in the summer as a short cut to the hills; most didn't survive. Even today, daytime travel in the summer (by foot or by car) is not advised.

Aside from its extreme heat in the badlands, Death Valley has snow-capped peaks, unique rock formations, and brilliant wildflowers. Even with less than two inches of rainfall annually, this dry area supports more than nine hundred kinds of plant life, including juniper, pine, and mahogany forests. Wildlife survives here but, understandably, most animals are nocturnal.

In the desert's southeast corner, Zabriskie Point offers a terrific view of the badlands. On a clear day Mt. Whitney can be seen—at 14,500 feet it's the highest point in the continental U.S.

In the northeast are sand dunes, which are particularly beautiful in the late afternoon when they change colors with the setting sun.

This page, top to bottom: In San Diego's Seaport Village, three Plazas recreate old-time villages. Tall ships add dignity and charm to San Diego's harbor. The Marriott Hotel wraps around the San Diego Harbor. Opposite: The old and elegant style of San Diego's train station contrasts with the clean and sophisticated lines of a modern office building.

Antelope Valley, in the Mojave Desert, bursts into bloom in the springtime. Below: Joshua trees bear clusters of white blossoms at the ends of their branches. Opposite: Rock formations in Anza-Borrego State Park.

Joshua trees and palm forests dot the landscape of Joshua Tree National Monument. Below: Joshua Tree National Monument lies between two deserts—the low Colorado and the high Mojave. This makes for a varied landscape, studded with dramatic trees and rock formations.

Preceding page: *Death Valley's badlands are deeply etched by wind and occasional cloudbursts.* This page, below: *Death Valley is distinguished by its low altitude and extreme temperatures, which can exceed 130 degrees Fahrenheit.* Opposite: *The highest point in Death Valley is Zabriskie Point's Telescope Peak, which rises over 11,000 feet above sea level.*

Index of Photography

All photographs courtesy of The Image Bank,
except where indicated *.

DEP. LEG. B-24.879-90